JEWELED BEARINGS

FOR

WATCHES

A FULL AND COMPLETE DESCRIPTION OF THE MANUFACTURE,
GAUGING AND SETTING OF JEWELED BEARINGS IN
TIMEKEEPING INSTRUMENTS

By CHARLES T. HIGGINBOTHAM
CONSULTING SUPERINTENDENT SOUTH BEND WATCH COMPANY
AND PAUL HIGGINBOTHAM

Copyright © 2013 Read Books Ltd.
This book is copyright and may not be
reproduced or copied in any way without
the express permission of the publisher in writing

British Library Cataloguing-in-Publication Data
A catalogue record for this book is available from the
British Library

A History of Clocks and Watches

Horology (from the Latin, Horologium) is the science of measuring time. Clocks, watches, clockwork, sundials, clepsydras, timers, time recorders, marine chronometers and atomic clocks are all examples of instruments used to measure time. In current usage, horology refers mainly to the study of mechanical timekeeping devices, whilst chronometry more broadly included electronic devices that have largely supplanted mechanical clocks for accuracy and precision in timekeeping. Horology itself has an incredibly long history and there are many museums and several specialised libraries devoted to the subject. Perhaps the most famous is the *Royal Greenwich Observatory*, also the source of the Prime Meridian (longitude 0° 0' 0"), and the home of the first marine timekeepers accurate enough to determine longitude.

The word 'clock' is derived from the Celtic words *clagan* and *clocca* meaning 'bell'. A silent instrument missing such a mechanism has traditionally been known as a timepiece, although today the words have become interchangeable. The clock is one of the oldest human interventions, meeting the need to consistently measure intervals of time shorter than the natural units: the day, the lunar month and the year. The current sexagesimal system of time measurement dates to approximately 2000 BC in Sumer. The Ancient Egyptians divided the day into two twelve-hour periods and used large obelisks to track the movement of the sun. They also developed water clocks, which had also been employed frequently by the Ancient Greeks, who called them 'clepsydrae'. The Shang Dynasty is also believed to have used the outflow water clock around the same time.

The first mechanical clocks, employing the verge escapement mechanism (the mechanism that controls the rate of a clock by advancing the gear train at regular intervals or 'ticks') with a foliot or balance wheel timekeeper (a weighted wheel that rotates back and forth, being returned toward its centre position by a spiral), were invented in Europe at around the start of the fourteenth century. They became the standard timekeeping device until the pendulum clock was invented in 1656. This remained the most accurate timekeeper until the 1930s, when quartz oscillators (where the mechanical **resonance** of a vibrating crystal is used to create an electrical signal with a very precise **frequency**) were invented, followed by atomic clocks after World War Two. Although initially limited to laboratories, the development of microelectronics in the 1960s made **quartz clocks** both compact and cheap to produce, and by the 1980s they became the world's dominant timekeeping technology in both clocks and **wristwatches**.

The concept of the wristwatch goes back to the production of the very earliest watches in the sixteenth century. Elizabeth I of England received a wristwatch from Robert Dudley in 1571, described as an arm watch. From the beginning, they were almost exclusively worn by women, while men used pocket-watches up until the early twentieth century. This was not just a matter of fashion or prejudice; watches of the time were notoriously prone to fouling from exposure to the elements, and could only reliably be kept safe from harm if carried securely in the pocket. Wristwatches were first worn by military men towards the end of the nineteenth century, when the importance of synchronizing manoeuvres during war without potentially revealing the plan to the enemy through signalling was increasingly recognized. It was clear that using pocket watches while in the heat of battle or while mounted on a horse was impractical, so officers began to strap the watches to their wrist.

The company H. Williamson Ltd., based in Coventry, England, was one of the first to capitalize on this opportunity. During the company's 1916 AGM it was noted that '...the public is buying the practical things of life. Nobody can truthfully contend that the watch is a luxury. It is said that one soldier in every four wears a wristlet watch, and the other three mean to get one as soon as they can.' By the end of the War, almost all enlisted men wore a wristwatch, and after they were demobilized, the fashion soon caught on - the British *Horological Journal* wrote in 1917 that '...the wristlet watch was little used by the sterner sex before the war, but now is seen on the wrist of nearly every man in uniform and of many men in civilian attire.' Within a decade, sales of wristwatches had outstripped those of pocket watches.

Now that clocks and watches had become 'common objects' there was a massively increased demand on clockmakers for maintenance and repair. Julien Le Roy, a clockmaker of Versailles, invented a face that could be opened to view the inside clockwork – a development which many subsequent artisans copied. He also invented special repeating mechanisms to improve the precision of clocks and supervised over 3,500 watches. The more complicated the device however, the more often it needed repairing. Today, since almost all clocks are now factory-made, most modern clockmakers *only* repair clocks. They are frequently employed by jewellers, antique shops or places devoted strictly to repairing clocks and watches.

The clockmakers of the present must be able to read blueprints and instructions for numerous types of clocks and time pieces that vary from antique clocks to modern time pieces in order to fix and make clocks or watches. The trade requires fine motor coordination as clockmakers must frequently work on devices with small gears and fine machinery, as well as an appreciation for the original art form. As is evident from this very short history of clocks and watches, over the centuries the items themselves have changed – almost out of recognition, but the importance of time-keeping has not. It is an area which provides a constant source of fascination and scientific discovery, still very much evolving today. We hope the reader enjoys this book.

JEWELED BEARINGS FOR WATCHES.

There has been no single improvement in watch manufacturing of so great a value to time keeping as the jeweled bearing, which has universally superceded the brass and gold plugs, or bushings which were formerly used and which were found very unsatisfactory because of friction, wear and corrosion. The honor of being the first to use gems—jeweled bearings—for watches is due to an Italian, Nicholas Facio, who after prolonged experiments and repeated failures finally succeeded, about the year 1723, in successfully applying them to watches, although the reader must not imagine that they bore any similarity to the watch jewel of today other than that the material was the same.

Instead of a hole piercing the jewel there was ground in one face a V-shaped depression (See Fig. 1) which made it extremely difficult to finish because of the tendency to form a tit at the bottom of the depression during the operation; furthermore such a shape was only suitable for V-shaped pivots such as are now found only in cheap clock movements. Nor must the reader imagine that the art of cutting precious stones was previously unknown, nor that up to the time of Facio, jewels had not been drilled, for such was not the case. Cutting gems had been extensively done and there is a record of a Roman architect, Vitruvius, who about the year 250 B. C. constructed a clepsydra in which was used a drilled jewel for the opening through which water, by which it was actuated, found egress.

Although the Swiss were quick to realize the advantages to be secured by jewelled bearings and began experimenting on their manufacture, the difficulty of making and polishing

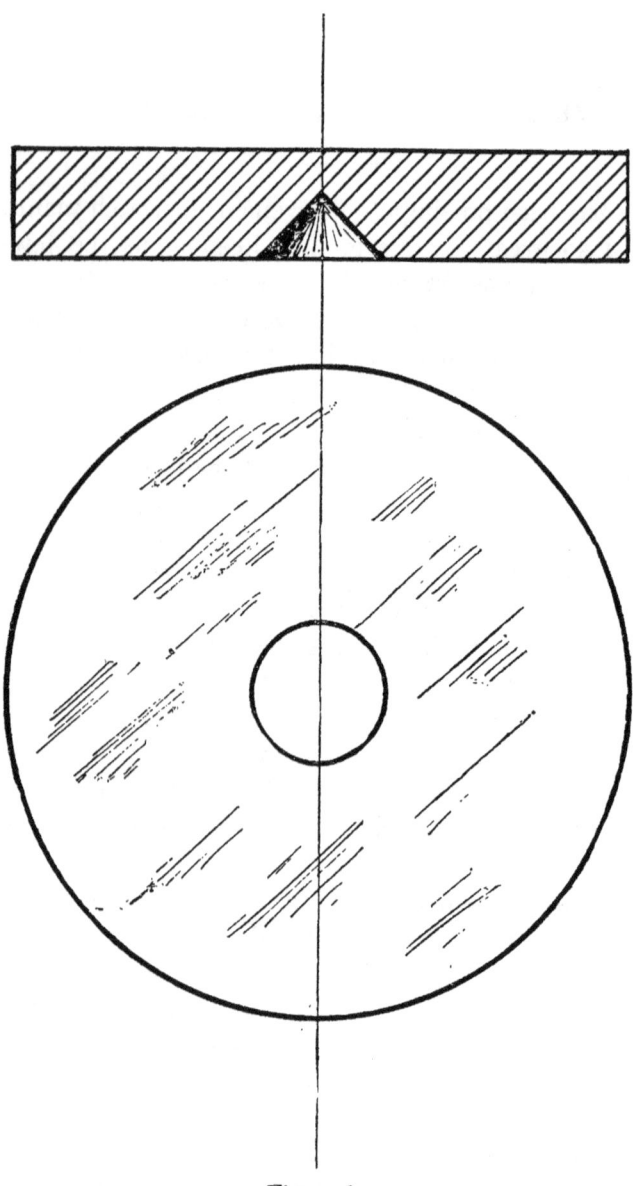

Figure 1.

a V-shaped depression without leaving, either a tit, or a flat bottom was very great, in fact practically insurmountable, so that not until about a century later did jewels for watches come into general use, and even then, only for the balance and escapement pivots. By this time the pierced jewel had superceded the V cup. The process of drilling and shaping such minute openings as are required for watch pivots was entirely new and was fraught with many difficulties. These difficulties required a long time to overcome, so that as late as the present century many great improvements in the method of manufacture have been made.

There are practically but four kinds of jewels used in the watches of today; namely, diamonds, sapphires, rubies and garnets, although aquamarine and chrysolite have been, and are now, used to some extent. What is known as diamond chips are used almost universally as upper and lower cap jewels for marine chronometers, and are growing in popularity with the makers of fine watches both in this country and abroad. The Swiss, however, have in many so-called "imitation jeweled watches" used diamond cap jewels for the upper alone, with a ruby or other stone for the lower, which together with the practice of jeweling only the upper train holes have won for them the name, "Imitation Jeweled." This practice has been carried to a still greater extent, in the custom of inserting garnet, and even glass endstones into recesses in the top plates where actually no pivots found bearings.

The balance of a marine chronometer being of considerable weight, and the instrument being run in such a position that the entire weight is sustained by the end of one of the staff pivots, this pivot is found very apt to wear a depression in any stone, even a diamond; and the moment this wearing or cutting begins, it goes on very rapidly, for the reason that the end of the pivot quickly becomes charged with particles of the stone; in fact when a diamond endstone begins to pit it cuts more rapidly than a sapphire. The pitting of endstones (commonly attributed to soft, spongy, or imperfect jewels) more frequently comes from quite another cause. At the time machine made balance staffs were introduced, the belief prevailed that the method of grinding the pivots with diamond laps charged the pivot end and was responsible to a great extent for pitted endstones. It has been demonstrated, however, that this is an error. Grinding a pivot which is properly tempered, with a diamond lap will never charge it. The writer has by extensive experiments and exhaustive tests proved to his own entire satisfaction that the main cause for pitted endstones is from improper hardening and tempering of the steel of which they are composed. It is a well known fact that diamond is crystalized carbon. Now when high carbon steel such as is used for balance pivots is overheated in hardening, the carbon which it contains becomes crystalized and forms minute particles that, if not actual diamonds, possess all the abrasive properties of the diamond itself, and will cut any stone, even a diamond. In experimenting along this line it was found that a staff made of steel rich in carbon, when heated to a white heat in hardening would cut an endstone in 24 hours. The same steel heated to blood red in hardening would not do so. The experiment was also tried of reheating a staff several times, the result being that as the carbon was more or less burnt out by repeated heating, the pivot became less and less liable to pit the stone.

The sapphire, we might say is, almost without exception, used for barrel arbor, or main wheel and for center lower jewels and is exceptionally well adapted for this use because of its superior strength and its minimum cost for stones of this size. It is also used for balance hole jewels and for cap jewels. Sapphires and light rubies are almost indistinguishable from each other, and are used indiscriminately, except in watches where the display of a higher colored stone for the upper endstone is desired, in which case the high colored ruby, known as the pigeon blood, replaces the sapphire, although it is a softer stone. Since the introduction and popularity of the double roller and steel escape wheel, sapphire roller pins—impulse pins—are used because of their superior strength, and sapphire pallet stones because the steel wheel will not cut that stone. In this connection let me say that a brass escape wheel tooth when acted upon by a sapphire pallet stone is extremely liable to cut, whereas, the same tooth acted upon by garnet, will not. Sapphire is aluminum colored with titanium and iron while ruby is aluminum colored with chromium, thus although they are nearly similar, there seems to be a chemical action set up when brass escape wheels are used with sapphire, also like action (though not so pronounced) when used with rubies; this is made apparent by causing excessive friction on the brass wheel, often cutting it quite rapidly and sometimes stopping the watch.

There are several sources of supply for the rough sapphires from which the jewels are cut, chief of which are Ceylon, Australia and Montana. They are found in about all colors of the rainbow. The Australian stone is the hardest and correspondingly brittle. The stone from Ceylon is not quite so hard, and is less brittle. The Montana stone is said to be best for jewels in mechanisms where any strength is required, as it is less brittle than the others, and therefore not so easily fractured. The stones commonly range in size from a diameter of about one-quarter inch to three-eighths inch.

The ruby besides being used for balance holes and endstones as above described, is well adapted for upper and lower plate holes, the high color—to make a distinction—being placed above the center, third, fourth, escape and pallet arbor, except in cases where some of these may be capped. or, as in the case with balance jewels, they may, in the lighter color, be of the sapphire family. Jewel pins are frequently made of ruby for higher grade watches, although ruby is not quite as hard. They are frequently used in highgrade watches for pallet stones on account of their beauty of color. The high-colored ruby is falling into disuse of late, for the reason that they are too soft to be satisfactory.

The garnet is of good color but very soft as compared with ruby or sapphire. It is used principally for plate holes in third, fourth, escape and pallets, but although it is less expensive, both in the rough and to manufacture, it is growing less popular every day, at least among American watch manufacturers; and is now principally confined to cheap watches. Garnets are much more friable than sapphires or rubies and for this reason entail a larger percentage of waste during the processes of manufacture, particularly in that of setting. Setting in recent years is done largely by automatic machines which not being endowed with that human quality called judgment, press just as hard on a thin jewel as a thick one. Garnets are, however, peculiarly adapted for use as pallet stones in connection with brass wheels, and in this connection are used almost exclusively.

JEWEL MAKING.—The requisite equipment for making a jewel consists mainly of tools found on the watchmaker's bench, together with a few others which are quite simple in construction. The lathe may be of any style, but must run true and be capable of high speed—say two thousand revolutions per minute. It should be equipped with a T-rest, a female taper chuck, together with a number of brass tapers to fit, a copper lap about 4 inches in diameter, an alcohol lamp, or a small Bunsen burner to which gas may be led by means of a rubber tube; also the following which it will be necessary to make: a diamond drill, a diamond cutter and a skive or jewel saw.

To make the drill, select a slender diamond splint tapering to a fine point; of course, only diamond chips or imperfect stones are used for this purpose. All diamonds used for this purpose are not of like value; those of dingy color usually make the best drills and cutters, the clear stones, while being very hard, are apt to be too brittle for this purpose. When a workman has secured a drill of the proper size, shape and quality, it becomes practically priceless. To make a diamond drill, drill into the end of one of the brass tapers a hole just large enough to take the splint and secure it by burnishing the soft brass against it. In addition to this the space between the diamond and taper may be filled with either soft, or hard solder. It is perfectly safe to apply any heat that can be developed by a blow pipe to a diamond. After being secured to place, the superfluous metal may be cut away. To give it the proper length and facilitate its manipulation, set the brass taper in a wood handle of any convenient size or shape. The cutter for turning the jewel is made in the same way, except that the splint is selected

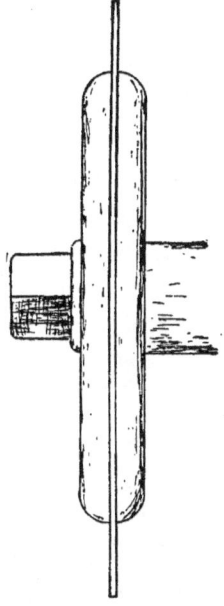

Fig. 2.

with a view of having a strong, somewhat chisel-shaped cutting edge. The skives used in factories are of large diameter, ten inches or more and are mounted in gangs, the individual skives being separated by discs of proper thickness, according to the jewel desired and that portion projecting beyond the flange is sometimes slightly dished. The described skives, of course, would be an impossibility on a small bench lathe, but for making one or two jewels, the lesser diameter will answer. The smaller tool will require more frequent charging. To make this, cut from a thin sheet of tin a piece, approximately round and of as large diameter as will swing in the lathe; drill a hole in the center of the proper size to make a fit on the saw arbor. Now make in the same way two discs an inch less in diameter than the tin; these may be either brass or iron and should be of sufficient thickness to give rigidity to the saw. Clamp these on the arbor with the saw between, making sure that it is true both as to flat and diameter. See Fig. 2.

To charge the lap, select a small hard pebble and while holding it to the edge of the skive apply drop by drop, diamond powder between them while revolving the skive slowly. As the skive charges it will cut the pebble more and more rapidly, but this may be obviated by applying different parts of the pebble. Another method is by using a roll of hard steel mounted to revolve freely in a suitable handle. This is brought against the edge of the skive with diamond powder applied between. The diamond powder used for this purpose may be quite coarse. No. 1 is none too fine. The copper lap may be charged by hammering the diamond powder into its face, but a more economical way is that of rolling in as has been described for the skive.

The tools are now ready to begin operations, but first we will describe the preparation of diamond powder, for although few watch repairers use it in sufficient quantity to make it practical from an economical standpoint to settle their own, still it is well to know how it is done. Diamond powder is made from diamond borts, or splints, by pounding them with a steel pestle in a steel mortar. The mortar is fitted with a steel cover which is usually threaded to screw into the mortar. Through the center of the cover a hole is made large enough to admit the pestle which is packed or surrounded with sheet rubber to prevent any of the small particles of diamond from being lost during the operation. See Figs. 3 and 4.

The diamond is broken into minute particles by striking the upper end of the pestle with a hammer. This is continued until the proper degree of fineness is reached which can be determined by frequently testing between the fingers. Considerable practice will be required to know when it has been ground enough, though it can hardly be ground too

Fig. 3.

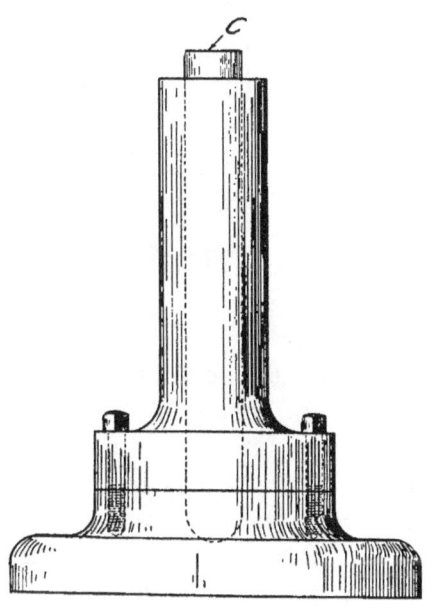

Fig. 4.

much, except that the longer it is ground, the more of the finer grades and the less of the coarser will be the result. After crushing sufficiently, empty the powder on a large sheet of fine surfaced white paper, taking care to gather all the dust and particles. Having previously secured a half dozen bowls with straight sides and rounded corners at the bottom, for the purpose of insuring a uniform settling and of facilitating the removal of the powder when settled (see Fig. 5) fill a bowl with oil. Olive oil is frequently used for this purpose, but I prefer clock or watch oil for the reason that it can be used over and over again without becoming rancid, whereas in using olive oil fermentation is likely to ensue, causing more or less waste of diamond powder. Stir

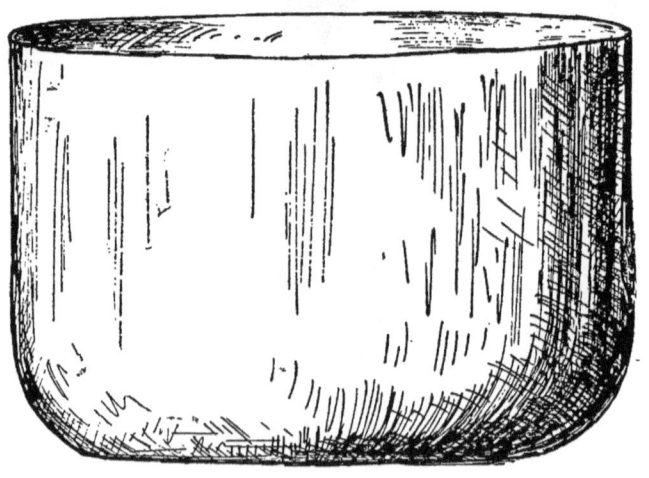

Fig. 5.

the ground powder into the bowl of oil. Allow it to settle for about 30 minutes and then pour off the top; which is to say all but the settlings, into one of the other bowls. Stir thoroughly that portion which has just been poured off and allow it to settle for an hour. Repeat as before and so on until there are five different settlings, the first and second having been 30 and 60 minutes respectively. The third should be allowed to settle four hours, the fourth ten hours and the fifth, not less than 24 hours, but preferably a number of days. The periods used for settling are varied from more or less, depending upon special requirements and special conditions of the oil used.

JEWELED BEARINGS FOR WATCHES. 13

The first, or No. 1, is the coarse or grinding powder, and the last, or No. 5, is the polishing powder. In watch factories No. 1 is used on laps, chiefly for grinding steel tools and watch parts, but for the ordinary watch bench, it would be well to continue the grinding of the powder in order to produce by far the largest per cent of No. 3, No. 4 and No. 5, No. 1 may be used for charging skives and laps as well as sharpening tools. In this connection let me say that the charged lap will be found an excellent and expeditious method for sharpening drills and other tools. The second, or No. 2, may be used on laps for grinding jewels and No. 3 on laps for polishing. No. 4 and No. 5 are used on laps usually of ivory, celluloid, African box-wood, tortoise shell and other substances. These laps are not charged, but have the diamond powder placed loosely upon them.

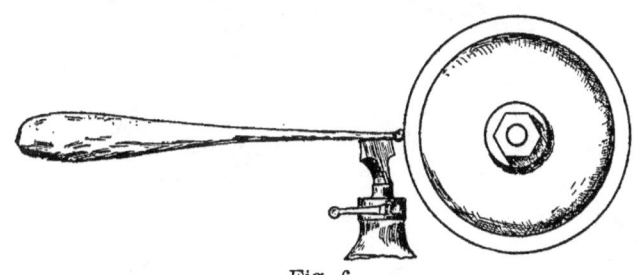

Fig. 6.

It sometimes happens that, after settling the powder, it has not been sufficiently crushed to give the proper grades, in which case cut the oil by adding benzine and after settling for five or six hours, pour off the top. This should be repeated and then the residue allowed to evaporate. The powder can then be placed in the mortar and reground.

JEWEL MAKING BY THE ENGLISH PROCESS.—The old English method of jewel making is as follows: The pebble from which it is desired to make the jewel is cemented on the end of a stick about 8 or 10 inches in length, shaped on one end to make it convenient to hold in the hand and tapering to the other end to approximately the diameter of the pebble. Place the skive in the lathe, adjusting the T-rest close to it, somewhat below the center and set the lathe in motion. The speed for a skive may be varied considerable. For ordinary use two thousand revolutions will be found to answer the purpose very well, but after some practice this speed may be increased considerably. Steadying the stick against the T rest, hold the jewel with a light pressure against the skive edge as illustrated, Fig. 6.

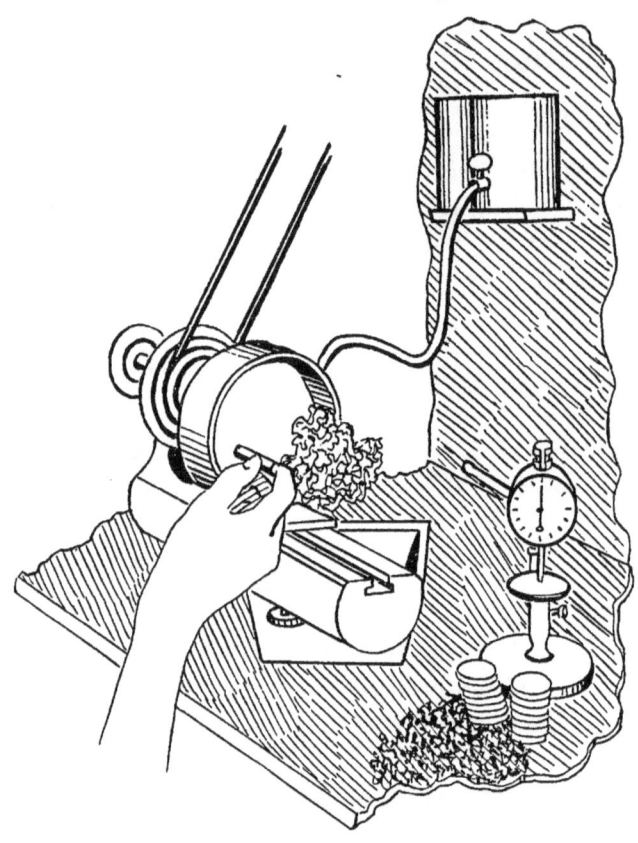

During the operation of cutting, in order to prevent overheating, oil should be frequently applied. This may be readily accomplished by suspending a sponge saturated with oil, on a piece of wire above the skive, so that it will come in contact with the edge. Make as many slots parallel to each other as the size of the pebble and the thickness of the jewels will allow, taking care that the distances between the slots—the thicknesses of the slabs—is somewhat greater than the thickness the jewel is to be when finished. When flaws are sawed into, or the slab is not flat the defective slabs may be saved frequently by lapping them down as illustrated. This is seldom advisable except for special jewels. Remove the slabs, clean the cement from them and mark off on one of them a number of squares large enough to allow for the diameter of the jewel, Fig. 7.

These squares may be laid out with a straight edge and deeply scratched with a diamond point. They may be broken

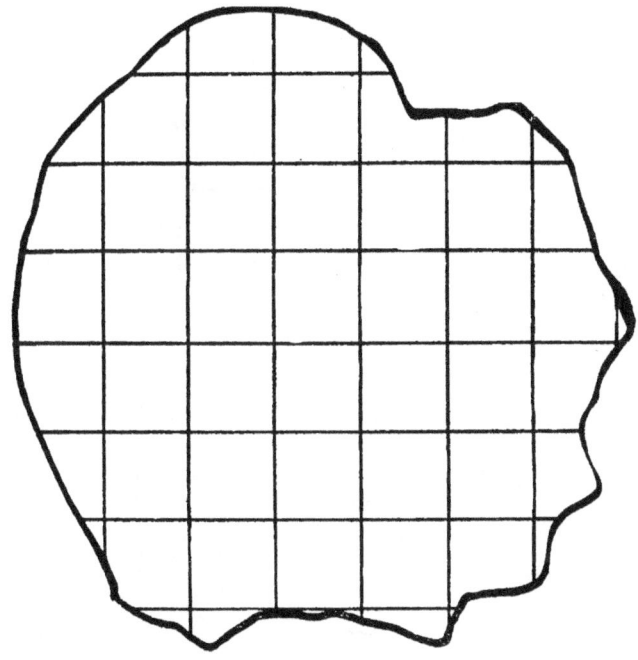

Fig. 7.

apart by the use of a pair of pliers padded with some soft metal. Now take one of these squares and chip off the corners with pliers until it is approximately round in shape. Place a brass taper in the lathe and true the end, cupping it slightly and turning the diameter to somewhat less than the finished diameter of the jewel. See Fig. 8. This figure shows the end of the taper which it is observed is turned to somewhat smaller diameter a short distance back, at A.

The object of this is to facilitate the heating of the end of the taper.

Let the lathe revolve slowly, at the same time heating the end of the brass taper by means of the alcohol lamp or Bun-

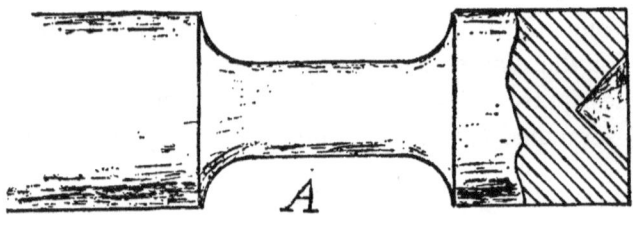

Fig. 8.

sen burner, until it is warm enough to melt shellac, which should be applied in a thin layer. Stop the lathe, and quickly —before the shellac has had time to cool and set—pick up the slab by pressing the end of a finger on it and apply it to the end of the taper. Start the lathe slowly, applying gentle

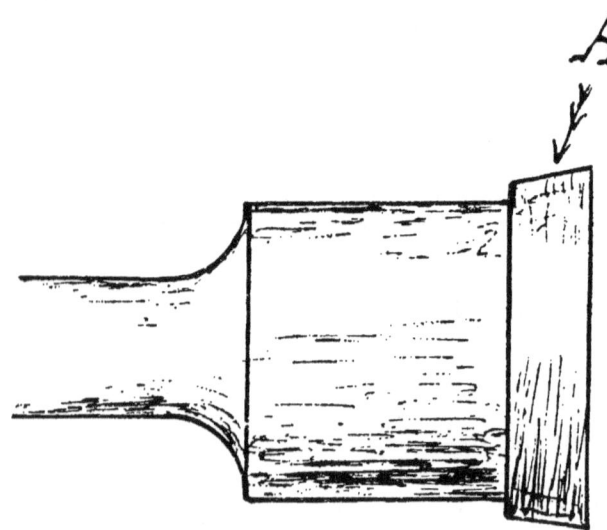

Fig. 9.

heat, and with a piece of pegwood touch lightly the outside diameter of the jewel until it runs true. Stop the lathe and press firmly with the pegwood against the face of the jewel until the shellac sets, which will take but a minute; then, with the diamond cutter, turn the outside diameter to the size intended for the finished jewel; then give a slight bevel from the front face to form the setting edge, as at A, Fig. 9.

The jewel is now ready for the drilling operation which will probably be attended with much difficulty and many spoiled jewels and broken splints, for it is no mean trick to

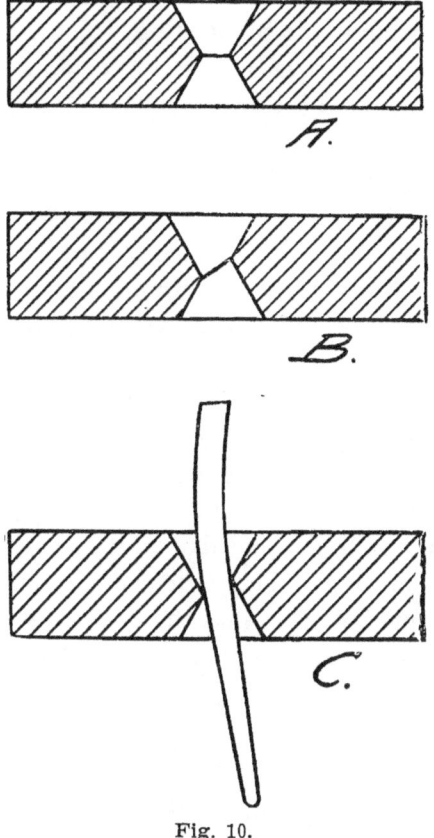

Fig. 10.

drill without forming a tit at the bottom of the hole. The hole should be drilled a trifle more than half through the jewel. When this has been done, remove the jewel and reversing it, cement the drilled side to the chuck or taper, being careful that it is trued up perfectly, this being absolutely necessary in order that the holes, drilled from opposite sides, may meet perfectly. Drill as before, but very slowly and carefully as the drilling from the other side is approached, for then is the greatest danger of breaking both drill and jewel. Fig. 10 will illustrate the condition sought to be secured in drilling from opposite sides. A is a jewel drilled correctly; B is one in which the drillings from opposite sides do not coincide. When a rough jewel is drilled as shown at B, it is well nigh impossible to secure a straight, or round hole by opening, for the reason that the wire opener will be more or less deflected as shown at C.

Before removing the jewel turn the convex curve of the outside, also the concave recess or oil cup. Polish and finish as follows: Turn a hollow in one end of a copper wire; form a rounded end on a piece of steel wire of the shape the outside of the jewel is intended to be—it is not necessary to harden the steel—drive the rounded end into the recess formed in the copper wire, thus securing the proper shape. Putting a little No. 3 diamond powder in the recess thus formed, bring it against the jewel and start the lathe running. Keep the copper wire constantly moving from side to side, the outer end forming an ellipse, frequently moistening it with oil in order to prevent heating. It may be necessary to add a little more diamond powder once or twice during the operation. The object of keeping the copper wire in constant motion is that the lines may be broken and a uniform surface free from rings be produced.

This should produce a very fine surface, almost amounting to a polish. Where a finer polish is desired it may be secured by turning a recess in the end of a small strip of African boxwood. Putting a little No. 5 diamond powder in the recess thus formed, bring it against the jewel and proceed as with the copper wire.

The oil cup is polished in the same way, except that the end of the wire, as well as that of boxwood, must be formed convex instead of concave. This will leave the circle where the concave cup and convex edge meet, sharp and somewhat ragged. Flatten this edge slightly with a strip of soft steel charged with No. 3 diamond powder; then polish it with a strip of boxwood and No. 5 powder. Now remove the jewel from the chuck and remove the shellac with alcohol. It is now ready for polishing the flat surface, which is best done by holding the jewel against the face of a lap with a light pressure of the finger. A boxwood lap is best for this purpose, and No. 3 diamond powder may be used, except where a higher finish is desired which can be secured by an additional operation—a boxwood or pine lap with No. 5 powder. Keep the jewel constantly moving while being presented to the lap. This precaution is necessary in order to produce a polish free from lines.

Fig. 11.

OPENING AND POLISHING THE HOLE.—It now remains to open the hole to the required size and to give it the proper form. This operation may be performed either before or after the jewel is set. The advantage of doing this after the jewel is set is that it is more readily held in a chuck. The disadvantage is that there is more or less danger of small particles of diamond powder used in opening, finding lodgment between the jewel and its setting, with the danger of its ultimately finding its way into the jewel hole. Whenever a balance hole is set before opening, it should always be removed and reset afterward. In removing the jewel, the setting may be dissolved off with muriatic acid which will not injure a sapphire or ruby jewel. A jewel may be opened before being set by observing the following directions: Take another taper and in the end of it turn a recess a trifle smaller than the diameter of the jewel, to a depth of about the thickness of the jewel. Saw two longitudinal slots at right angles to each other through the center of the taper, running back about half an inch. Fig. 11. This forms a spring chuck into which the jewel is pressed and will hold it, if carefully made true.

The opening of a sapphire or ruby jewel is best done with a soft steel wire which should be filed to a slight taper. The less the taper the better. This may be charged by placing diamond powder on a hard steel surface and rolling the opening wire on it by means of another hard steel surface. This is to say, roll the opener between the two surfaces. In

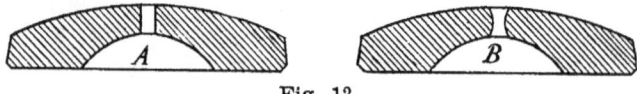

Fig. 12.

using this opener, soap is better than oil as a lubricant. A small piece of soap kept moist with water should be at hand and the opening wire drawn through it from time to time. An opening lathe should run at a speed of not less than two thousand revolutions per minute. In using the opener, it should be inserted in the hole at a slight angle and a continual (but very slight) side to side motion of the wire used. Care should be exercised to avoid pressing the wire tightly into the jewel being treated, as this is apt to result in a broken jewel. When an olive hole is desired, the angle at which the opener is entered should be greater than when the hole is to be straight. It is also well when opening for an olive hole to reverse the jewel in the chuck from time to time. The difference between an olive hole and a straight hole is shown in Fig. 12, where A is a straight hole and B an olive hole. It is a common impression that an olive hole creates less friction than a straight one, but this is an error. The length of a bearing has nothing to do with frictions.

The resistance caused by friction, as applied to a balance pivot, is determined by the weight of the balance and the distance of the surface in contact from the center (the diameter of the pivot) and is entirely independent of the amount of surface in contact. The advantage of an olive hole is that when oiled there is less adhesion of oil between the inner wall of the jewel hole and the pivot. If a balance could be run without the use of lubricants it would revolve just as freely when its pivots had their bearings in a straight, as when in an olive hole. Fig. 12 shows the difference between straight and olive. A is a straight hole, B an olive.

The usual range of watch jewel sizes runs from 1 to 3 millimeters outside diameter, the holes for the pivots ranging in the different sizes, say from 7/100 to 40/100 millimeters, or, from about 0.003 to 0.016 inch.

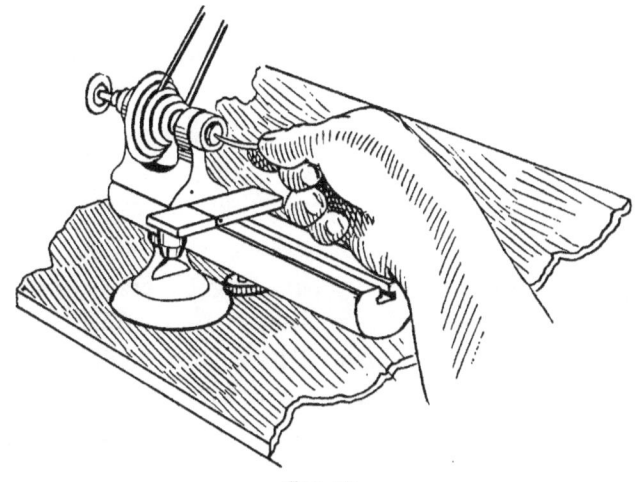

Fig. 13.

After the jewel has been properly shaped by the opener, it should be polished. The polishing is most frequently done with a long, pointed piece of pegwood which has been rolled in No. 5 powder. Sometimes a slim, pointed piece of tortoise shell is used for a polisher, but a still better one is made by dressing a piece of goose quill to a long, slender taper. This material is extremely tough and flexible; hence, its superiority. For olive holes, I do not know of its equal. When presented to the jewel at an angle, its flexibility causes the inner as well as the outer part to lie against the curved margin of the hole, producing as near a perfect polish as can be secured. I recommend this especially in treating balance jewels for adjusted watches.

For opening holes in softer jewels, such as garnets, a copper wire is quite as good, possibly better, than a steel one. In this case it is not necessary to charge the wire. No. 4 diamond powder may be used by simply applying it to the opener, which charges itself when brought in contact with the jewel hole.

When the jewel hole has been opened and polished, there remain two final operations; that of chamfering both front and back. The chamfering is done with a copper wire, the end of which should be cone shaped. No. 4 diamond powder is best for the purpose. The object to be secured is to form a slight chamfer in order to take off the sharp edge where the hole and surface meet. Great care should be exercised in treating the inner or flat side of the jewel, for the reason that if the chamfer is too deep it may allow the chamfer usually made on a staff to enter, thus increasing friction.

JEWEL MAKING ACCORDING TO THE SWISS PROCESS.

The Swiss method of jewel making differs in many particulars from the English method. In cutting the rough stone into slabs it is cemented to a short strip of leather. This leather is held on a table directly under the skive: the table being moveable upward. It is thus brought against the under edge of the skive, the leather being moved along as slab after slab is cut. Each slab is then cemented to the leather and passed along under the skive, cutting it into strips. These strips are broken into smaller pieces and brought to an appropriately round shape by chipping the edges. In doing this chipping, the stone is laid on a flat surface and the edge chipped off with a hard, angular pointed instrument. The stone is then cemented to the chuck in a manner similar to that used by the English and the similar operations carried on until the process of drilling is reached. Here is the main difference between the English and Swiss methods.

As has been explained, the English pierce the jewel with a diamond splint, piercing from both sides, whereas the Swiss drill with a steel drill, penetrating the jewel completely in *one operation*. The drill has its end charged, usually with very coarse diamond powder. It is made quite short to guard against deflection. The lathe is run at a very high speed and the drill is also carried by a spindle running at a high speed, but in the opposite direction from the lathe. This method is a much quicker one than the English splint drilling. In using the wire drill it is rarely necessary to drill entirely through the jewel. When the drill nears the inner face, the operative, with a sharp thrust, breaks out the remaining stock, the jagged depression left being shaped when the cup is made. The jewel is now cemented on the reverse side and the subsequent operations performed in a similar manner to the English method. Ordinary sizes of jewels are regularly turned, drilled and polished at the rate of 80 to 100 in a day. The holes in these jewels can be drilled and polished by one operator at the rate of 200 per day.

INSPECTING.—American watch manufacturers import nearly all their jewels, either direct or through a jobber. If imported direct, they have arrangements with the maker whereby they return, after examination, all jewels of faulty construction or poor material. In fact this is the general practice, even when purchased through the medium of a jobber or importer. The jewels thus rejected are generally placed upon the market at considerably reduced prices. They belong in the same category as imitation American watch material, and are to be avoided by workmen who take pride in their work and desire the best results.

The inspection in American watch factories is usually conducted as follows: A number of jewels, from one hundred up, in proportion to the number comprising the lot being inspected, are examined minutely in every particular. Should more than three or four defective jewels be found, the entire lot is returned, but in any event each individual jewel is inspected. After being inspected, those accepted are put through a series of sieves, each having a number of holes. These holes are of a uniform diameter in each sieve, but diminish by gradations, the uppermost sieve having the largest holes, the difference between the sizes being 1/1000 of an inch. The sizes embraced by these sieves determine the limit of sizes to be accepted. Such jewels as will not pass through the uppermost sieve, and such sizes as do pass through the lowermost are rejected. Those which are within the limits are kept separate as to sizes, to facilitate setting. This is absolutely necessary where automatic machines are used for the process.

It is well that the repairer should understand what constitutes a good jewel.

The stock, that is the stone itself, should be perfectly uniform in color and free from flaws, air bubbles, or other defects of that character, its texture showing the characteristic uniformity of a perfect stone. The setting edge should be thick enough to give a firm hold when the stock is burnished over it. An excessively thin edge is exceedingly liable to fracture in the process of setting. How often a jewel is found set in a watch, showing chips in the outer edge! This is the result of a thin edge, or poor workmanship in setting. The edge should be of a uniform thickness all round. Otherwise it will not be possible to set it flat. Another condition as to shape is the convex side. This is practically an arc of a circle. If the radius of this arc is too small, the jewel will be, so to speak, bullet shaped, and inasmuch as this curved surface must rest against a shoulder of the setting when the jewel is burnished in, it will be seen that it would be very difficult to burnish in a jewel so shaped and yet have the face perfectly flat and true with the setting. Some jewel setters prefer to have the edge slightly tapered, while others prefer it straight—at a right angle with the face, but this is solely a matter of choice, which does not affect the excellence of the jewel. Another point to observe is that the hole shall be vertical with the flat face of the jewel. Where this condition does not exist it is technically called an "out of straight hole." Fig. 14.

In this figure the condition is somewhat exaggerated, it being so done to make the nature of the defect clear. Sometimes this defect is not discovered until the gaging of the hole size is being done, when it is found that the jewel will tilt to one side. Finally the jewel is inspected for exterior

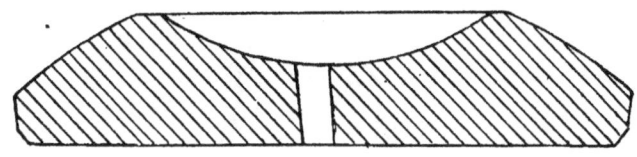

Fig. 14.

finish, finish of the hole, shape of the hole and its chamfering. A jewel hole should be either perfectly straight, or more or less olive shaped. The difference between straight and olive has been previously explained. An olive-shaped hole will allow of a closer side shake than a straight one for the reason that the least want of conformity between the pivot and jewel will make a great difference where a straight hole is used. The pivot and the sides of the hole must be absolutely parallel where a close side shake prevails in a straight hole, and even then the adhesion of oil proves a serious drawback. Fig. 15. This figure shows two jewels in connection with two pivots identical in size. It will be seen that the pivot fitted to the straight hole cannot be tilted to the same extent as that fitted to the olive hole, without binding. What is known as a "thin hole" is another fault often found in jewels. The term, thin hole, does not in reality pertain to thickness, but to length, as will be seen by comparing jewel A with jewel B, in Fig. 16. In a balance jewel a thin hole is a serious fault, frequently resulting in the cutting of the balance pivot.

Holes out of center—not central with the outside of the jewel—are extremely common and sometimes cause much trouble. This defect in a jewel itself, provided no other one accompanies it, can be remedied by what is known as

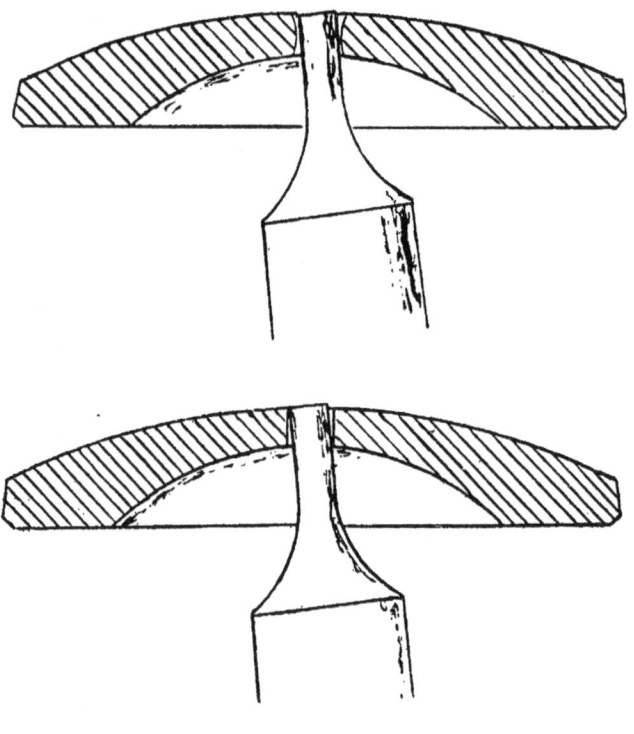

Fig. 15.

"shellac truing," which will be described later on. Chipped holes are apt to be very disastrous, but may be readily discovered. By chipped holes is meant that a portion of the face of a jewel is broken away into the hole, which will sometimes cut the shoulder of the pivot.

Still another defect is known as "ringed face." Where this defect exists, scratches, more or less deep, surround the hole. It is usually caused by the point of the opener striking the face during the process of opening.

Finally, in the matter of inspection, the countersink, particularly at the face of the jewel, is carefully examined. This countersink should be just sufficient to take out the

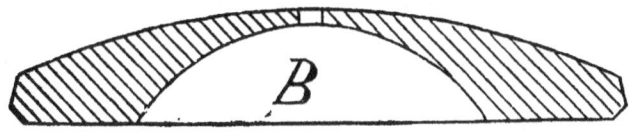

Fig. 16.

sharp edge and such minute chips as may be occasioned by the process of making and opening. The expressions, making and opening, are used for the reason that they indicate two entirely different operations. The countersink is sometimes extended in order to cut out larger chips; this is a very bad practice. It gives a smaller bearing for the pivot shoulder, in some cases even letting the beveled portion of the staff down into the countersink, thus causing a wedging pressure which is, of course, disastrous to timekeeping.

Fig. 17 shows a train jewel and a balance jewel, both of correct shape in every respect. A jewel so shaped may be readily set and will produce superior results as to friction, retention of oil, etc.

Before leaving the subject of jewel inspection, it is well to say a few words about stratification. Stratification refers to what may be termed the grain of the stone. All precious stones, even the diamond, are formed in crystalline layers. They have a grain like wood, although this is not apparent

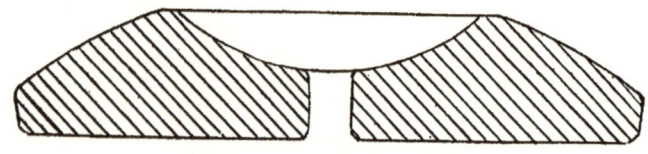

Fig. 17.

to the ordinary observer, even under a magnifying glass. The diamond cutter, however, frequently acquires a keenness of observation which will enable him to detect it. This is of great assistance to him in his business, inasmuch as it is necessary to present a diamond to the lap with its line of

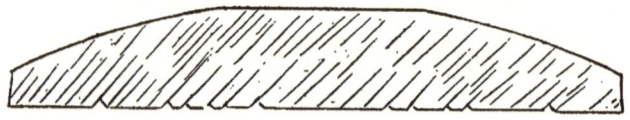

Fig. 18.

cleavage (grain) parallel with the circle described by the lap in running. In watch jewels the lines of cleavage are sometimes, though not as a rule, perceptible. When they form an angle with the flat face of an endstone, the angular portions of these lines will sometimes chip off in minute particles, thus charging the pivot. Fig. 18. This figure is designed to show what is meant by the angles formed by the lines of cleavage chipping off. It will be understood that the drawing exaggerates the condition.

In some factories jewels are gauged and sorted out in a variety of thicknesses in order to facilitate the setting where automatic machinery is used for this purpose.

JEWEL SETTING.—Where automatic machinery is used for setting jewels, the wire which forms the setting is usually fed out automatically and after the jewel is set the wire is cut off to the proper length; but where they are set by hand, the settings are previously prepared. The process of setting, being to all intents and purposes, identical in both cases, we shall describe the latter.

In all American watch factories jewel settings are made on automatic machines. The shape of a jewel setting is

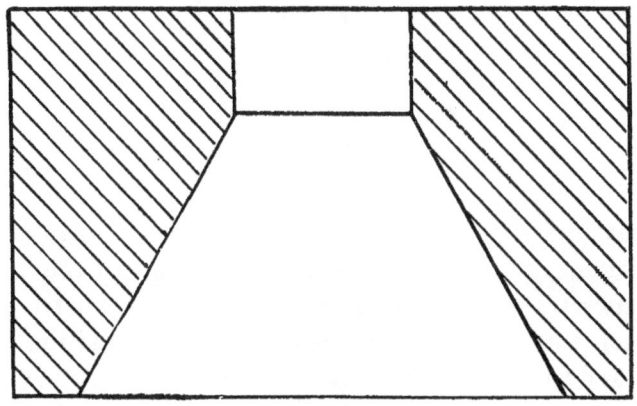

Fig. 19.

illustrated in Fig. 19. The object of having the hole at one side of a V shape is solely for the purpose of facilitating the subsequent process of stripping, by leaving less stock to be removed in the operation. In the process of setting, a step chuck is used. The setting is placed in this chuck with the V opening toward the lathe spindle. Fig. 20. This figure shows a portion of the chuck holding the setting in position, the shape of the cutter and form of the recess made by it for the reception of the jewel. A is the chuck; B, the jewel setting; C, the cutter. The jewel to be set is placed between the jaws of a caliper rest, thus insuring the making of the recess of a proper diameter to fit the *outside* of the jewel. This is a very important matter for the reason that if a jewel does not completely fill the recess it is very likely,

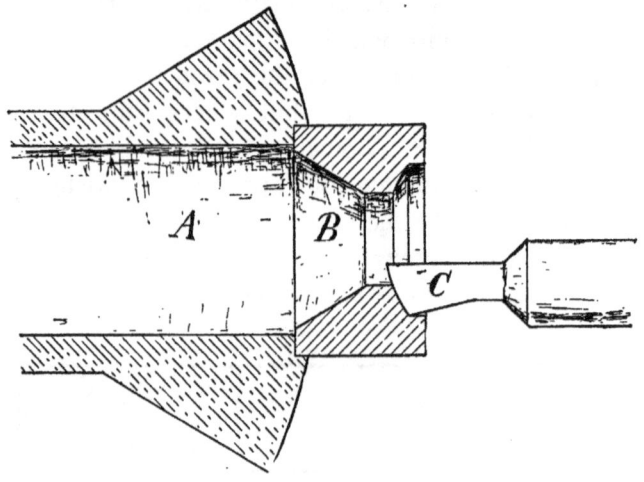

Fig. 20.

when burnished in, to be out of center with its setting. This is to say, the jewel hole will not run true nor will the outside diameter of the jewel. The disadvantage of this is that it necessitates shellac truing, which is a somewhat tedious operation and one requiring considerable skill. If the jewel is true and the hole central, it can be burnished into a setting, and the setting then trued up before removing from the chuck, the result being a perfectly true jewel and setting.

Fig. 21 gives an enlarged view of a cutter for cutting the seat in a jewel setting, the jewel setting with the seat cut, and the jewel in place ready for burnishing. Pick the jewel up on the end of a finger slightly moistened and place it in the recess face out—we refer to a train jewel (bar hole). It is now ready for burnishing. Burnishing (or rubbing in) as it is called, is an operation requiring judgment and skill which is only acquired by practice. The shape of the burnisher and the manner of presenting it are essential features to the success of this operation.

In Fig. 22 we have endeavored to show in detail the manner of procedure. A is an edge view of the burnisher. B is a side view. C is a jewel setting with the jewel in place;

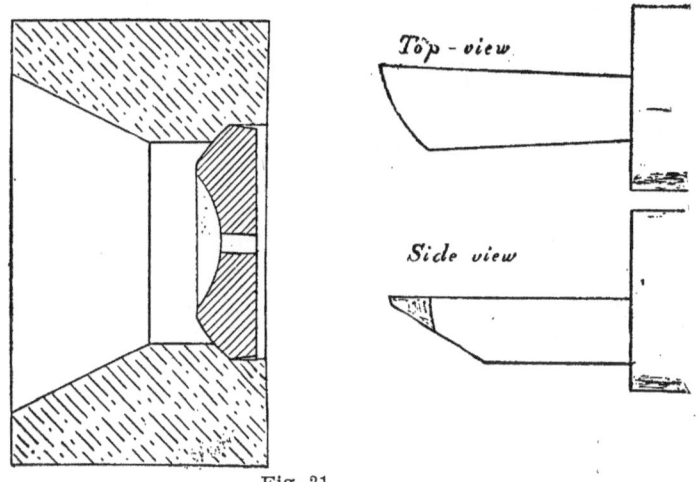

Fig. 21.

the first operation of burnishing has been done, and the burnisher is in the exact position while doing the work. It will be observed that the burnisher has been forced into the brass of the setting a certain distance from the recess; further that it has been forced down until its point has penetrated to a distance equaling the depth of the recess in the setting. This has separated a portion of the stock from the main body except at the inner side. This little ring of metal is now to be laid over against the edge of the jewel. For this purpose cant the burnisher to one side as shown at D. The operation must be performed carefully in order to avoid cutting through the ring. The stock should be laid over slowly, gradually canting the burnisher during the procedure. The ring of stock is now in position for the final burnishing operation. This is represented at E. It will be seen that the upper part of the stock has been burnished over close against the jewel. We have described the operation of burnishing as well as we could and trust it will give the novice the correct idea as to the necessary manipu-

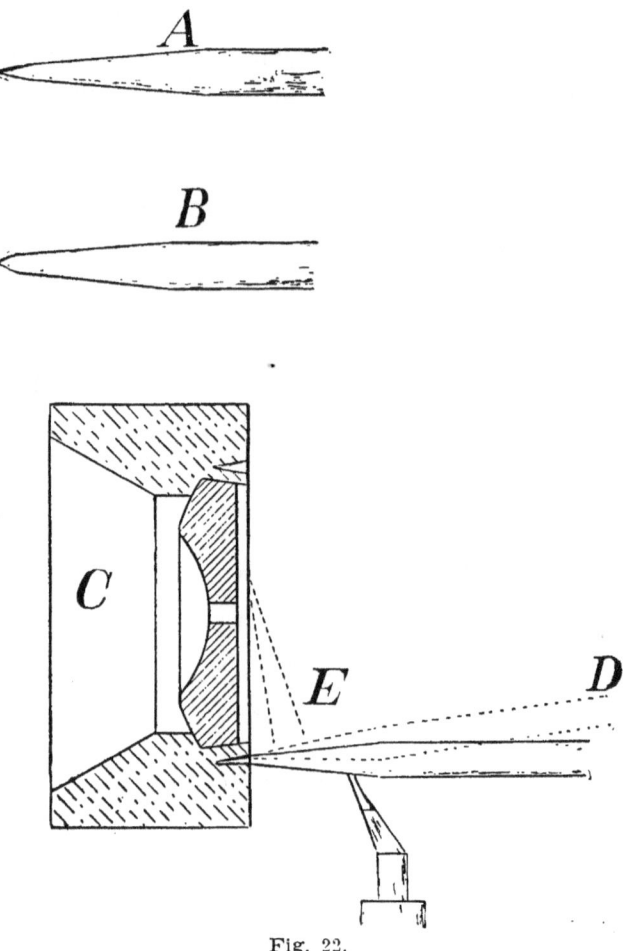

Fig. 22.

lation. It would be advisable for him to secure a few imperfect jewels for the purpose of practicing the operation. All factories have, of necessity, more or less waste jewels which are of little value to them and could be readily secured at slight cost. Speaking for one of those factories, the South Bend Watch Factory of South Bend, Ind., we are

JEWELED BEARINGS FOR WATCHES. 33

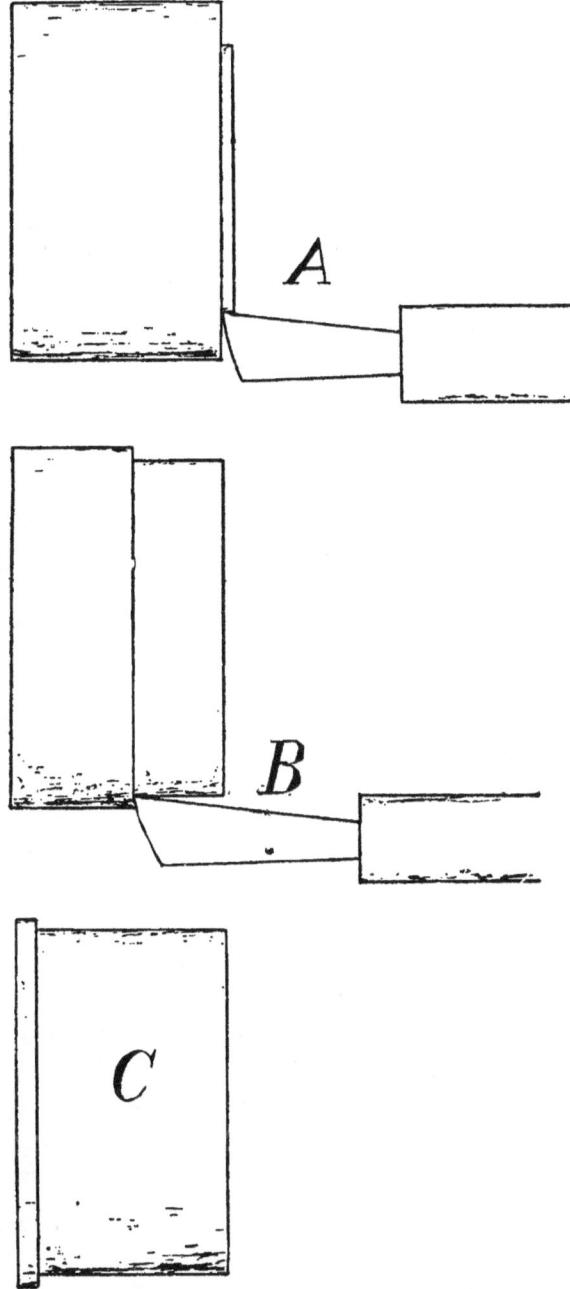

Fig. 23

authorized to say that they will be supplied gratis upon request.

The jewel having been burnished—rubbed in—the next operation is facing the setting—cutting the setting flat and true with the jewel. For this purpose use a cutter as at A, Fig. 23, passing it across the setting from the outside. This leaves a perfectly flat face coinciding with the face of the jewel. A cutter, as at B, is now passed over the edge as shown. The jewel when removed shows a setting with a slight rib, as at C. This rib, it will be understood, is the part held in the chuck. Now, it will be understood, that the recess in the setting and the outside of the setting run perfectly true with each other; therefore if the jewel has been set true and the jewel hole is central with its outside, the jewel and setting as a whole is true, and it only remains to cut off the rim. This is a simple operation. Place the jewel in a

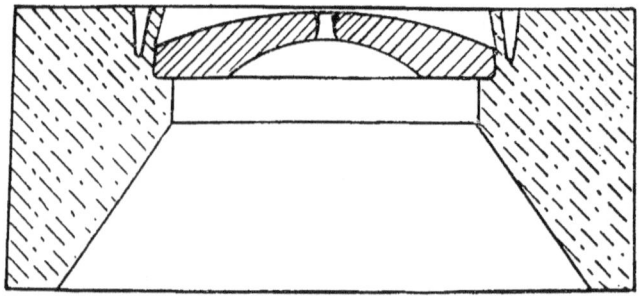

Fig. 24.

chuck—preferably a step chuck—and remove it by passing a cutter across or turning it off with a graver.

The process for setting a balance jewel is mainly the same, the differences being that the bottom of the recess is flat, Fig. 24, and the face of the jewel—the cup side—rests against it, the burnishing being done against the convex side.

SHELLAC TRUING.—Shellac truing is a somewhat difficult operation and is only used, when owing to imperfect setting or imperfectly centered jewels, the hole is not central

JEWELED BEARINGS FOR WATCHES.

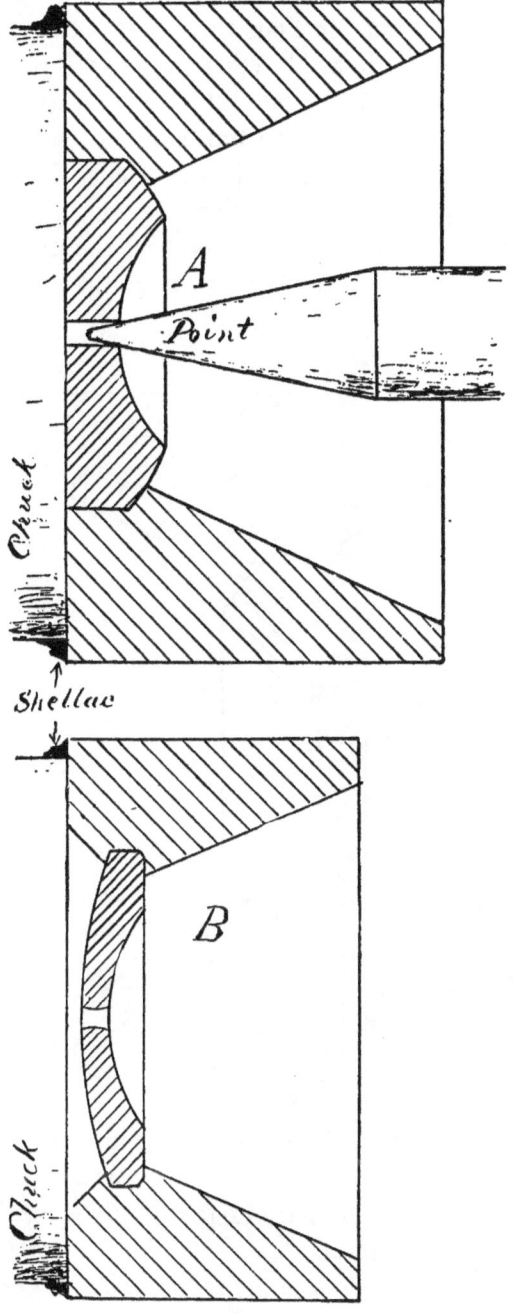

Fig. 25.

with the setting. In shellac truing the end of the taper is turned somewhat smaller than the jewel setting. The setting is cemented to it as shown in Fig. 25. Shellac is applied to the end of the taper and the face of the setting brought in contact with it and the hole made to run true by inserting a point as at A, while the shellac is cooling. A shows a train jewel and B a balance jewel, giving the correct position with regard to the end of the chuck. When the shellac is cool, a cutter passed over the edge will true up the setting.

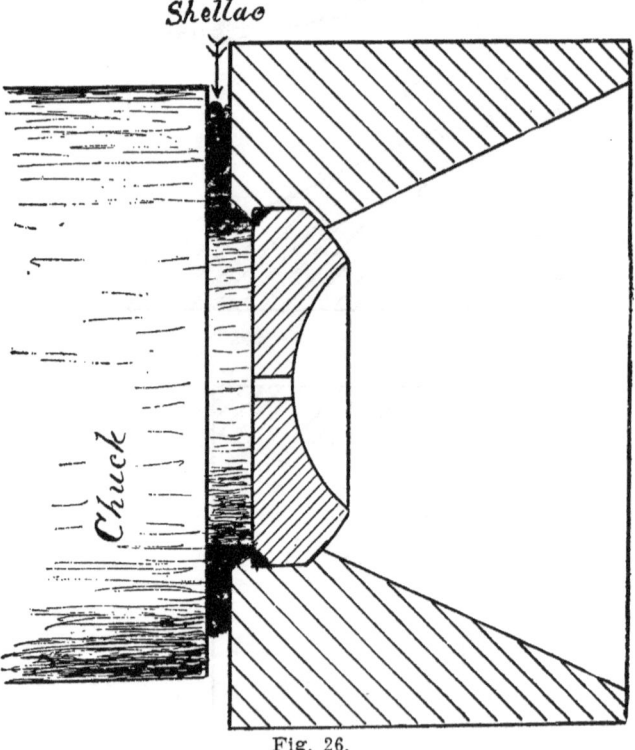

Fig. 26.

It sometimes happens that a jewel, owing to an imperfect setting edge or to some other radical defect in the jewel itself, cannot be set so that its face will be perfectly flat with the setting. In such case it is better not to use the jewel; it can never be made a perfect job. If, however, it is absolutely necessary to use it, it can be to some extent

JEWELED BEARINGS FOR WATCHES. 37

remedied as follows: Turn the end of the taper small enough to contact with the face of the jewel without touching the setting. This is best accomplished by turning it with an exterior step as shown in Fig. 26. The object of turning it to this form is that it affords a better hold for the shellac than

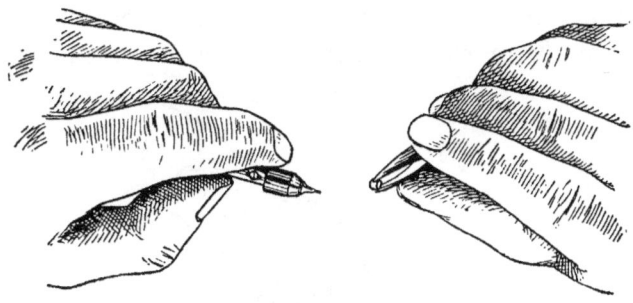

Fig. 27.

if the taper were turned down to the diameter of the extreme end. This process is only practical for jewels having flat faces. There is too much uncertainty connected with the operation to make it advisable for balance jewels. The first method described, however, for shellac truing, is applicable

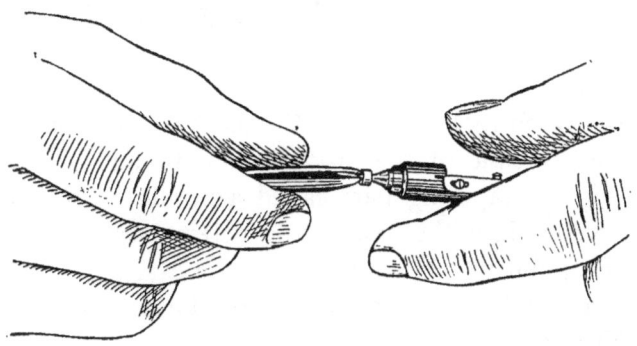

Fig. 28.

to all kinds of jewels having centrally located holes. When a shellac trued jewel has been previously inspected for finish, it requires no further inspection for centering.

JEWEL FITTING.—We have followed, throughout, the method of preparing the jewels and settings, to the point of applying them in the watch. We will now explain the method of selecting them to fit the parts, and **of securing** them in the watch plates.

Of course the first operation is to select a jewel having a hole of the proper size to give a sufficient amount of side shake for the pivot. This selection of course is determined by the eye, but it will be found a great convenience to have your assortment of jewels gauged and kept consecutively in sizes. For this purpose, a needle gauge, which can be pur-

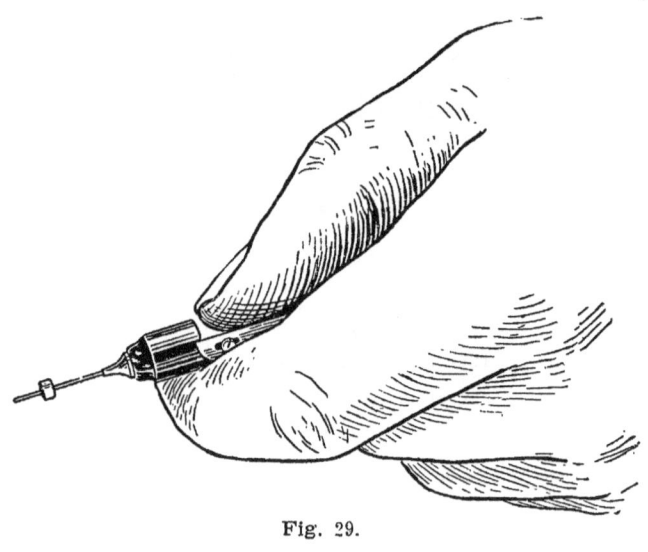

Fig. 29.

chased of watch tool dealers, is the most convenient tool to use. The principle of the instrument is that it is supplied with a slightly tapering part called a needle. This needle being inserted into the jewel hole determines the size by means of a point which is attached to the base of the needle, and is read on an index provided for the purpose. Some little skill and practice is required in the use of this gauge, especially if it is for gauging balance, or other small holes. There is considerable danger of breaking the needle if not used very carefully.

Figs. 27, 28 and 29 show the needle gauge and method of using it. Hold the gauge in the left hand with the thumb nail on the indicator point which slides along the index. Draw it down until the point of the needle projects slightly beyond the gauge as shown in Fig. 27. Take the jewel setting, or jewel in the tweezers as shown in the same figure. Insert the point of the needle into the jewel hole and slowly release the indicator point as shown in Fig. 27. Now draw the needle point down and with the tweezers press against the jewel, *lightly,* holding it against the end of gauge, release the needle. To remove the jewel from the needle after gauging, it is simply necessary to draw the indicator point back slowly, when the jewel will be released.

Having selected a jewel which has the proper sized hole, the next operation is to set it in the plate. In some watches jewels are set directly in the plate. This is accomplished precisely the same as when set in a setting, so far as the operation of rubbing in is concerned.

The watch plate is secured on the face plate of the lathe, the hole or location for the jewel being properly centered; the recess is made and the jewel then burnished in; observing the same directions as apply to jewel settings. When a jewel thus set becomes broken, it must be replaced with a jewel having the same outside diameter, or else the recess should be sufficiently enlarged to take a jewel with a much larger diameter; in fact, one with a diameter of sufficient dimensions to allow the recess to be made for its reception beyond the rib, or depression, made in setting the other jewel. It will be seen, therefore, that it is much better, whenever practicable, to replace a jewel set directly in the plate by one set in a setting.

In preparing the seat for the jewel secure the watch plate to the face plate of the lathe with its inner side toward the face plate as shown in Fig. 30. Center it up properly. The recess is then made for the jewel setting. It consists of two parts, the jewel seat shown at A, and the jewel body shown at B. It is best to have the jewel body portion as deep as possible in order to give stability to the jewel. The seat need only be of slight depth. One one-hundredth of an inch is usually quite sufficient.

The jewel setting has two parts called the pipe and the body. The pipe is the smaller portion shown at A, Fig. 31. The jewel body is the larger portion shown at B. The portion B, Fig. 31, should be a good fit for the plate portion B, Fig. 30. The pipe need not be a fit for the plate portion A. It is now necessary to provide the proper endshake for the pinion or arbor being jeweled. Let us assume that the jewel being fitted is in the lower plate. Place the pinion or arbor with its upper pivot in the top plate, lower side uppermost; invert the lower plate and put it in place with the lower end

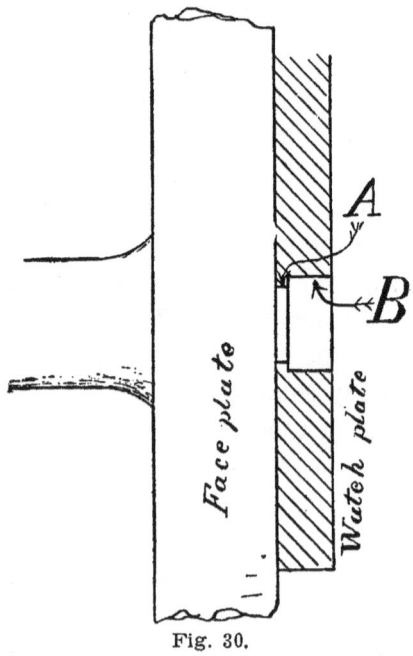

Fig. 30.

of the staff projecting into the recess made for the new jewel setting. Screw the plates together. Push the new jewel into place and try the end-shake. It will be seen that it is always best to cut the shoulder, or pipe, on the setting shorter than required in order that the end-shake when first tried may be too great, rather than too little. Assuming that it is too great on first trial, hold the jewel with its setting in a spring chuck and turn the shoulder back a trifle, repeating this until the correct endshake is secured.

SIDE-SHAKES AND END-SHAKES.—The measurements given are metric and are expressed in millimeters. Thus, .015 mm. is one and a half hundredths of a millimeter, .007 mm. is seven-thousandths, or nearly three-quarters of a hundredth of a millimeter.

For the convenience of those who may not be thoroughly conversant with metric measurement let it be understood that it requires, practically, two and a half hundredths of a millimeter to equal one-thousandth of an inch. To convert millimeters into inches multiply by .03937. Thus, two and a

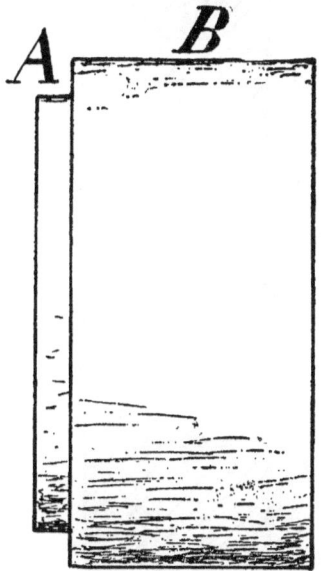

Fig. 31.

half hundredths of a millimeter, expressed .025 mm., multiplied by .03937, gives .00098425 inches.

The side-shakes and end-shakes given below are the result of repeated tests and careful observation covering a period of more than half a century and will be found to give excellent results.

In determining the proper side-shake and end-shake to give to any member of a watch train or escapement the shape of the jewel holes, the shape of the pivots and even the material of which the jewels are composed exercise an influence. A straight hole requires more side-shake than an olive hole. A cone pivot may be fitted with much less side-shake and end-shake than a straight pivot. This is to say, a pivot that is end-shook against its shoulders. A garnet or other soft jewel cannot safely be fitted as closely as a ruby or sapphire.

For all pocket watches, down to and including 12 size, the center, third and fourth may have .015 mm. side-shake and .04 mm. end-shake; the escape .01 mm. side-shake and .035

Fig. 32.

mm. end-shake; the pallet arbor .007 mm. side-shake and .035 mm. end-shake; the balance .003 mm. side-shake and .02 mm. end-shake.

For sizes 10 and below: Center, third and fourth, .015 mm. side-shake and .035 mm. end-shake; the escape, .009 mm. side-shake and .035 mm. end-shake; the pallet arbor, .006 mm. side-shake and .03 mm. end-shake; the balance, .003 mm. side-shake and .02 mm. end-shake.

For 19 and 21-jeweled watches where escape and pallet arbors are jeweled in olive holes the side-shakes may safely be made as close as the balance.

It may sometimes happen that in attempting to get the end-shake the shoulder may be turned back a little too much. This is sometimes remedied by holding the setting in a spring chuck and throwing up a slight burr on the edge of the shoulder with the pressure of a burnisher against it. This, however, is not to be recommended, being at best a makeshift, not a strictly workmanlike job. The outer end of the setting is now turned down slightly below the surface of the watch plate and its outer edge slightly chamfered, or brought to a taper as shown in Fig. 32; then the plate is burnished over to hold it, exactly as though it were a naked jewel being burnished into a setting.

In fitting a setting to a top plate proceed in the same manner up to the point where the end-shake is secured. Settings are sometimes put in by the method known technically as "frictioned in." This frictioning is sometimes done from the top side and sometimes from the lower side. I would advise against adopting this method except in case of dire necessity, and by all means never friction in from the top. The reason for this advice is that when a jewel is frictioned from the bottom there is at least no danger of its dropping out of the plate, which is not the case when frictioned from the top; but the disadvantage in both cases is that there is no certainty of the end-shake remaining permanently correct.

The only secure method of fastening in a jewel and setting which is desired to be removable from a plate, is to use two or more screws. We will now proceed to describe the method of accomplishing this. First we will describe the method of providing for securing the jewel where it has not previously been fitted in this manner. The first operation is to drill and tap two holes, diametrically opposite as to the jewel setting. These holes should be as near as possible to the recess without danger of bulging inward. In fact, it is better to make them before the recess in the plate is opened to its full size. This for the reason that the tap is less liable to bulge the wall out into the recess. The jewel being fitted is turned down almost flush with the upper side of the plate—say within 1/1000 of an inch—and one jewel screw brought to place with its head resting on the plate and projecting over the edge of the setting. This single screw will serve to hold the setting in place while counterboring the opposite hole for the screw head. Of course if the screw heads are to be left above the setting, this counterboring will not be done.

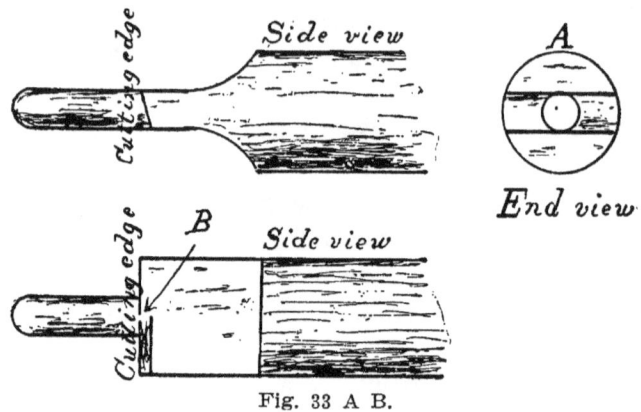

Fig. 33 A B.

There are two kinds of counterbores used for making recesses for jewel screwheads. One is known as the two-lipped and the other may be called the multiple tooth. A two-lipped counterbore is shown at Fig. 33. It needs no further explanation. Such counterbores may be bought of watch tool dealers or can be very easily made. In making a counterbore of this kind select a piece of steel wire of the size required for the recess. If this is not at hand select a piece somewhat larger in diameter; then turn down one end to the proper size; turn the point to a diameter that will just fill, without binding, the tapped hole for the screw. Now file two sides flat and parallel, as shown by the end view, A, Fig. 33. In backing off the lips the backing off should be carried around the tip of the counterbore, as shown at B. This counterbore is only suitable in cases

where there is no counterbore already in the plate; this is to
say, where no screwed in jewel has previously been used.
The multiple tooth counterbore is the proper form to use in
replacing a jewel having a screwed in setting. This form
of counterbore is shown in Fig. 34. In this figure, A is an
erd view, B a side view and C a view showing the position
in which the file should be held in making the teeth. A
counterbore of this form possesses the advantage that one or

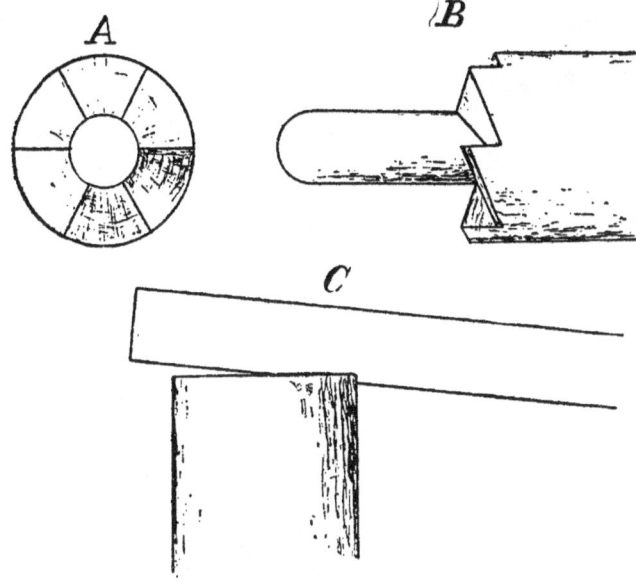

Fig. 34 A B C.

more teeth are always in action on the setting. Another advantage is that the cutting edge of the tooth is radial. The
method of making this counterbore is as follows: Proceed
as in the case of the lipped counterbore, to turn the outside
diameter the required size for the jewel screw head; drill a
hole in the end, of the exact size for the tit; shape the teeth
with a three-cornered or beveled edge file as shown at C;
harden the counterbore; turn up and fit the pilot, or tit;
finally fit a suitable handle. In order that the screw head
may hold the setting down to its place, the edge of a counterbore of this sort should be so shaped that it will cut a re-

cess slightly deeper at the center than at the outside; or at least it must not be deepest at the outside. The object of this precaution should be obvious. In order that a screw head may hold the setting down firmly to place the edge of the setting should be at least as high as any other part of the bottom of the recess.

In recessing for the jewel screw proceed as follows: The jewel being held in place by one screw, as previously described, insert the pilot of the counterbore in the hole at the opposite side and cut down the sctting to the depth required.

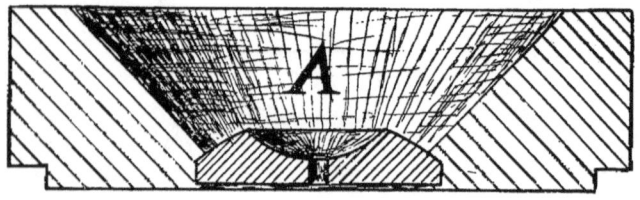

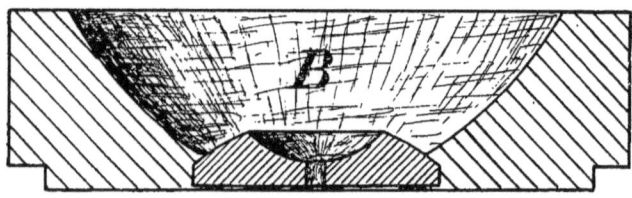

Fig. 35.

Now insert a screw into the recess just made and screw it in, to hold the setting; remove the screw first put in, cut the setting on that side and replace the screw. The operation is now complete so far as fitting the jewel is concerned.

STRIPPING AND POLISHING.—The technical term, "stripping," is applied to the beveled portion of the setting, whether this beveled portion be on a top plate, or a lower plate setting, or whether it be on the plate itself, where the jewel is rubbed directly into the plate. It is not usual to polish these bevels, except in the top plate. Balance jewel settings are sometimes polished. Train jewels in the lower plate are seldom polished.

The operation of stripping is a delicate one, requiring some practice. The stripping bevel is made in two different forms, known as straight bevel and concave bevel. Fig. 35 shows the two forms, A being the straight, B the concave. The form selected is entirely a matter of choice. The bevel should first be formed with an ordinary graver. This is called rough stripping. It is then finished, either with a sapphire stripping tool, or a polished graver. In watch factories the finished stripping is generally done with a sapphire tool. The form of this tool is shown in Fig. 36. The method

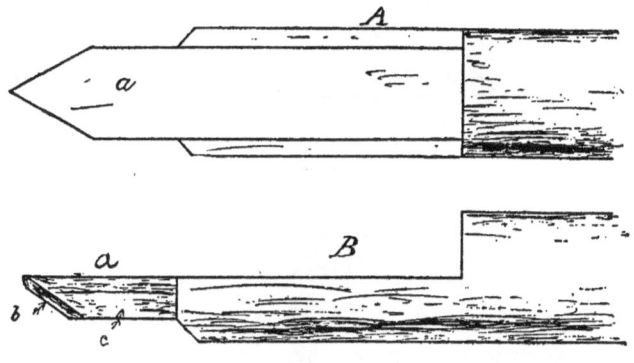

Fig. 36.

of making this tool is first to grind the sapphire strip to the proper shape, using a soft steel or copper lap charged with No. 1 diamond powder. These sapphire strips may be purchased in the rough. After bringing the cutter to form, it is then polished with a boxwood, or other hard wood, lap charged with No. 4 diamond powder. By finally finishing with No. 5 a very superior edge will be obtained. In the use of this cutter a good deal depends upon the manner in which it is presented to the work. The clearance edge should be held as nearly parallel with the bevel as possible.

Referring to Fig. 36, A is a top view; B a side view; a is the face; b the clearance, and c the undercut. It will be observed that the clearance edge b is slightly circular and forms but a slight angle with the face, a. This is essential for perfect work.

Where a concave bevel is desired, the point of the tool should be slightly curved.

The use of the sapphire stripper requires a great deal of practice, and is not to be advised except where the replacing of jewels is so frequent that the workman is enabled to keep up this practice. Almost as good results may be secured with a polished steel graver, and much more readily. To

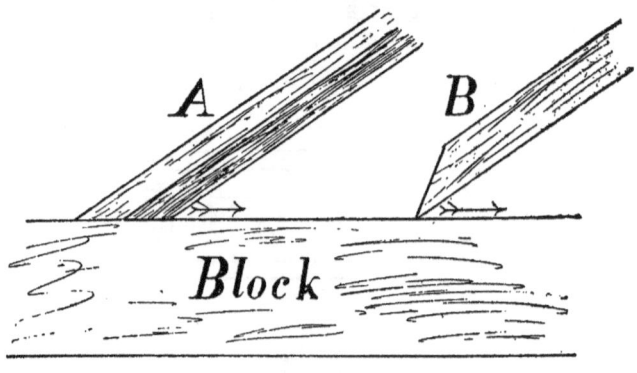

Fig. 37.

prepare this graver it should first be sharpened on an oil stone, observing the same care in shaping the clearance edge as in the case of the sapphire cutter. After sharpening to form, it should be polished on a boxwood or other close-grained, hard wood block, using Vienna lime and alcohol, or diamantine and oil; the former is the quickest and best. Fig. 37 shows how a graver should be presented to the block while being polished. A shows the position while polishing the face and B the position while polishing the clearance edge. The graver should be drawn from the cutting edge, as indicated by arrows, and the lines broken by a side-way motion. The same directions are applicable to the clearance edges. Instead of using a flat block, a hard wood lap may be used.

The polished graver described will not leave the finish of the bevel perfect. This may be done with a peg-wood point as shown in Fig. 38. This point is first dipped in alcohol and then in Vienna lime brought to impalpable powder. A and B indicate the shape of the peg-wood point. A gives

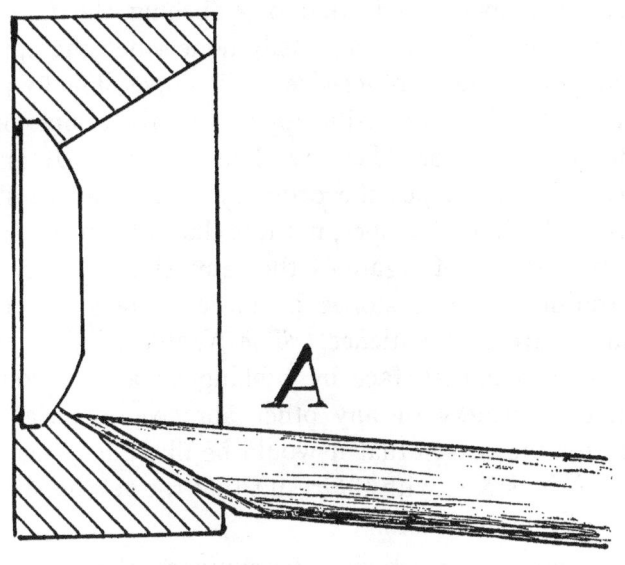

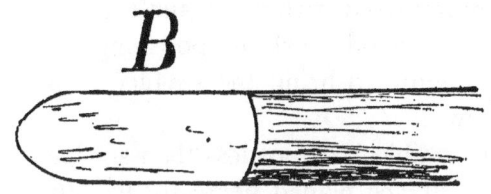

Fig. 38.

a side view and B an edge view. A is the position in which it is held while polishing the bevel.

In using the stripping tool, the polished graver, or the peg-wood polisher, care should be exercised that they be not held in one position during the operation. Constant motion is required in order to produce a perfect polish, and a freedom from lines. This is to say, the tools should first be brought with their points almost in contact with the jewel, then drawn slowly outward. Care should be exercised to avoid actually touching the jewel with the stripper, or the polished graver, either of which would be likely to scratch it; but the peg-wood polisher can do no harm. A little practice will enable the workman to acquire the necessary skill and produce a nice job of stripping.

The final operation is that of polishing the face of the jewel setting. This is very easily done when the appliances are in good order; otherwise it is impossible to produce good work. The requisite appliances are a fine piece of "water of Ayr," or "Tam O'Shanter" stone of any convenient size or shape; the ordinary 1-inch square slip will answer. A piece of Jasper, not less than 2½ inches in diameter, and a piece of Agate of the same size, or larger. The preparation of these stones is not extremely difficult, but requires care and patience. The Water of Ayr stone is brought to a fine surface by rubbing on a cast iron block. Do not use emery or any other abrasive material on the block, for the reason that it would be likely to penetrate the grain of the stone, with the result that the setting would not be free from scratches.

The method of preparing the surfaces of the Jasper and of the Agate are similar. These stones are found in the market already prepared with a flat surface, but not in condition to produce good work in polishing settings. The manner of procedure to bring the surface in proper condition is as follows:

Take a cast iron block of not less than six inches in diameter; have the surface planed perfectly flat and as smooth as possible, place upon the block a small quantity of very fine carborundum, or corundum mixed with oil—the former is best for the purpose. Either of these compounds should be of fine and uniform texture. This condition may be secured by *settling,* as in preparing diamond powder. The stone to be prepared should be rubbed on this block with a circular motion and a comparatively light pressure, until a perfectly true surface is secured on the stone. Now, the stone and block should be washed and wiped dry and the rubbing continued without any of the abrasive compound.

A repetition of these operations is desirable where the best results are expected. The last operation should be continued until the surface of the stone has a glassy appearance.

The final operation is known as charging the stone, for which purpose diamond powder is used. The term "charging the stone" is used in connection with the assumption that the grains of diamond powder are actually driven into the grain of the stone, but this is a matter of dispute which never has been definitely settled. However that may be, diamond is the only substance that has been found satisfactory. In charging the stone, a small piece of agate with a flat surface is used. This is called the charging stone, and is usually about an inch and a half in diameter. Its surface should be prepared by the same process as described for the larger jasper and agate stones.

For charging, use the finest settled diamond powder procurable. This may be obtained from the oil used in settling, as follows: After the No. 5 diamond powder has been procured by settling for 24 hours, allow it again to settle for at least five days; the residue thus obtained will be found excellent for the purpose of charging. Place a small quantity of this powder on the stone to be charged and rub with a small circular motion and light pressure of the charging stone. The result will be a beautiful, almost polished, surface. Now wash the stones thoroughly with grain alcohol and they are ready for use. In using them proceed as follows: Rub the face of the setting on the Water of Ayr; wash thoroughly and rub first on the jasper, then on the agate. If the stones have been put in proper condition a very few rubs will suffice. All these operations should be performed with a slight circular motion. For the final finish on the agate a heavy pressure is first used, gradually becoming lighter and lighter. In polishing, the bare finger should not be allowed to come in contact with the face of the stone. Fabric of some sort should be interposed. A finger-cot made of canton flannel, nap side towards the finger, is convenient to use for this purpose.

The stones used for polishing and that for charging should be taken great care of. Dust should be excluded, and they should be thoroughly washed with alcohol before using.

The author has gone into the various operations connected with jewel making, opening, setting and finishing, with considerable detail. In case anything in the above is not clear to the reader, or if further information on the subject is desired, a letter to the publisher will bring a prompt reply.

The shape of the balance jewel hole is of the first importance. The best results cannot be obtained where a hole having parallel sides is used for the reason that a very slight thickening of the oil will impede the motion of the balance unduly.

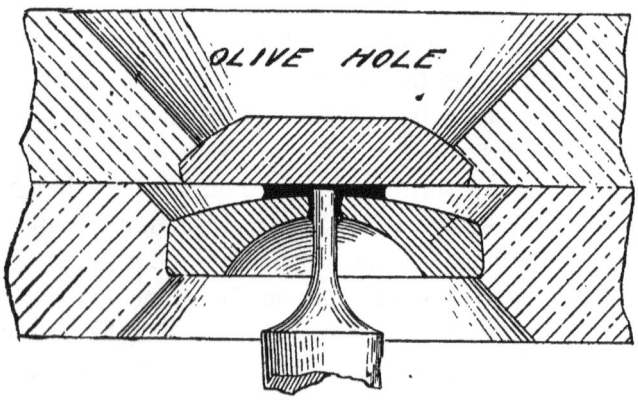

Fig. 39.

They should be what is known as olive holes as represented in Fig. 39. This shape reduces the retarding effect of thickening oil to the minimum. The face of the jewel should have a hemispherical oil cup and the back should be well rounded. When in position, the distance between the jewel and the endstone should be about two hundredths of a millimeter. If this distance is too great the jewel will soon become dry for a reason which I will explain a little later on. It is a very bad practice to allow the jewel and endstone to be in actual contact, as you will sometimes find in the cheapest foreign work. This prevents the oil flowing freely about the end of the balance pivot, where it is most needed. The advantage of having the back of the balance jewel well rounded and at a slight distance from the endstone is that the balance pivot will by this means be supplied with oil from capillary attraction.

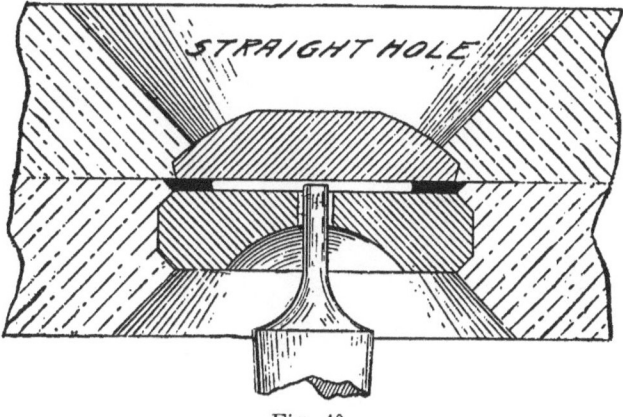

Fig. 40.

If the upper side of a balance jewel be flat, as shown in Fig. 40, the greater portion of the oil will be drawn between the settings, leaving the pivots dry, whereas, if the jewel be well rounded, the oil will collect at the center and the balance pivots be kept lubricated until the last particle of oil is exhausted.

www.ingramcontent.com/pod-product-compliance
Lightning Source LLC
Chambersburg PA
CBHW022121090426
42743CB00008B/956